YOUR KNOWLEDGE HAS VALUE

Junaid Javaid

Recommendations on Service Design & Delivery Case Study

GRIN Verlag

Bibliografische Information der Deutschen Nationalbibliothek:

Die Deutsche Bibliothek verzeichnet diese Publikation in der Deutschen National-bibliografie; detaillierte bibliografische Daten sind im Internet über http://dnb.d-nb.de/ abrufbar.

Imprint:

Copyright © 2013 GRIN Verlag GmbH
Druck und Bindung: Books on Demand GmbH, Norderstedt Germany
ISBN: 978-3-656-74806-9

This book at GRIN:

http://www.grin.com/en/e-book/281111/recommendations-on-service-design-deli-very-case-study

RECOMMENDATIONS ON SERVICE DESIGN & DELIVERY CASE STUDY

SHR608-6: ORGANISING MODERN HEALTH CARE SERVICES

WRITTEN & SUBMITTED BY:

JUNAID JAVAID

DATE OF SUBMISSION

25-MARCH-2013

EXECUTIVE SUMMARY

This report is written on the topic of care service design and its delivery pattern. The scope of this report is very broad as it has been focused on the Recommendation-1 outlined in the Mid Staffordshire NHS Foundation Inquiry report. This report based entirely on the Recommendations which I proposed to the Care Trust to follow on the timely manner as currently the Patients' Trust ranked higher in term of mortality rate and also categorised as poor in delivering standard services to all patients. As a Board Director of Trust I have analysed that Trust's patients are facing the significant problems (understanding the treatment options, getting brief explanations about their medications, not having access to the critical information and not receiving responsive and compassionate service from the Trust or Caregivers). And all of these issues are arising due to the failure of the trust in categorising the care service standards which has diverted their intention to other matters rather to focus on their patients' need first. In order to resolve the problem regarding to the care service design and its delivery pattern and also to improve the patients' satisfaction, I proposed the Trust to implement Patient-Centered Healthcare system. This system would allow the Trust to enhance the respect level for their patients' values and preferences which would also create awareness of quality of life issues among the care taking staff members. There are about seven factors (Leadership, Strategic Vision, Involvement of Patients, Supportive Work Environment, Systematic Measurement, Quality of Physical Environment and Supportive Technology) which would be contributed a lot to the success of Patient-Centered Healthcare System. The Trust must have to pursue certain strategies which would assist Trust in implementing Patient-Centered Healthcare System on authentic basis. These strategies are classified into two groups. The first one would strengthen the Trust capacity to accomplish Patient-Centered Care at the Organisational level. And the second group would meant to alter external reward in the Healthcare system which then guided the Trust to achieve the delivery of high standards care services to their patients. it has been concluded the Trust must have to build consensus in implementing the Patient-Centered Healthcare System and also needed the special effort from its management and staff members in attaining the key factors of this approach at the organisational level. So in this way Patients' Trust would able to get rid of care service delivery problem.

Table of Contents

1. Introduction

This report is comprised of different sections (Background Context, Aims & Objectives, Problem Statement, Recommendation and Conclusion) but the most important sections of this report are problem statement and recommendation section. This report based mostly on the synopsis of these sections. The recommendation section will be the center of focus for the Patients' Trust as it would enable them to get rid of ongoing issue of service delivery standards and design. The recommendation section will be composed of two parts, in the first part the proposed system will be explained along with its certain contributing factors which would give the Patients' Trust a competitive edge within the Healthcare services sector. On the other hand, the second part would recommend the Patients' Trust with certain strategies which must be pursued at both organisational and system level in order to make implementation of the proposed system possible and without any flaws.

The next section will review the concept of Health care services in depth, which thus would allow the reader to understand the importance of care service within the context of Health Care sector and how its successful design and delivery method would impact on the performance of the Healthcare Institutions which is normally measured through their patients' satisfaction and loyalty with given institution or trust.

2. Background Context

In general, the centre for health care service is perceived as the place where people come in a need to acquire services in term of assessment, diagnosis, treatment, rehabilitation and prevention from the Health-related problems. Hence these services can be provided at the three different levels (Primary, Secondary & Tertiary). In short, the Health Care Centres should always be intended to deliver services of high class standards to all patients by prioritising their patients' needs at the top level. It has been patented that the health care service is directly linked up with patients' well-being and should intended to enhance the current health status which can only be measured through the Patients' Satisfaction.

The Healthcare Trusts are basically follows the philosophy of establishing a partnership between its practitioners and patients (sometime include their patients' families) to ensure that the services provided to them are in accordance with the needs, wants and preferences of their patients. And on the other hand the patients must have an education and a support which thus needed by them in making decision and also to participate in their own care as well.

There are several studies which have shown that the healthcare institution which are basically oriented towards the approach of satisfying their patients' needs and preferences have the potential to increase their patients' satisfaction level not only with the delivery of superior healthcare services but also with the clinical outcomes as well. It would also permit them to lessen the both states (under or over use of medical services).

3. Aims & Objective

I'm writing this report to the Trust Board as Board Director in order to resolve the ongoing issue of Trust failure to prioritise the delivery high class care services to all of its patients. The core objective of this report is to suggest Patients' Trust a framework through which a Trust would able to get rid of care service delivery problem and thus would intended them to improve their patients' satisfaction not only with their care but also with their clinical outcomes as well. The other objective of this report is to suggest the Patients' Trust some strategies which would enable it to implement the system in the timely manner and also would be contribute the Trust to the important attributes of the proposed framework.

4. Problem Statement

From the inquiry report of Staffordshire NHS Foundation, it has been understood that patients are facing the significant problems (understanding the treatment options, getting brief explanations about their medications, not having access to the critical information and not receiving responsive and compassionate service from the Trust or Caregivers). And all of these issues are arising due to the failure of the trust in categorising the care service standards which has diverted their intention to other matters rather to focus on their patients' need first.

The next section will suggest the system through which the Trust would able to offset the recognised problem and thus would enable the Trust to remain aware about all of its patients' need which would also allow them to measure the standard their care services in the actual manner.

5. Recommendation

In order to resolve the problem regarding to the care service design and its delivery pattern and also to improve the patients' satisfaction, I'm as a Board Director proposed the Trust to implement Patient-Centered Healthcare system. This system would allow the Trust to enhance the respect level for their patients values and preferences which would also create awareness of quality of life issues among the care taking staff members (Institute-of-Medicine, Crossing the Quality Chasm: A New Health System for the 21st Century, 2001). And thus would be resulted in making them to remain attentive about the patients' needs and autonomy. So in this manner the Trust would able to deliver care services of high standards to all of their patients (Institute-of-Medicine, Envisioning the national health care quality report, 2001). The next section will briefly discussed the system of Patient-Centered Healthcare along with its key attributes, whereas the section thereafter will outline certain strategies which must be pursued by the Trust in implementing the proposed model of Patient-Centered Care.

5.1. What is Patient-Centered Healthcare System?

Conway, et al. (2006) stated that yhis system is emphasised more on providing and delivering both care and social services (including health, education, social services and mental health). According to some Scholars it is regarded as an innovative approach intended towards the planning, evaluation and delivery of healthcare which is being implemented as the outcome of mutually beneficial partnership existing among the healthcare patients and their providers (Gerteis, 1993; IPFCC, 2006).

5.2. Key Success Factors of Patient-Centered Healthcare System

There are about seven factors (Leadership, Strategic Vision, Involvement of Patients, Supportive Work Environment, Systematic Measurement, Quality of Physical Environment and Supportive

Technology) which would be contributed a lot to the success of Patient-Centered Healthcare System. These factors are briefly discussed below:

5.2.1. Leadership

It is the most import factor of Patient-Centered Healthcare System (Shortell, 2005). The reason of its importance is that the organisational transformational needed to accomplish the sustained and competitive delivery of patient centered care service which could not be happened without the support and the aggressive participation of top leadership (Schein, 1992).

5.2.2. Strategic Vision

The trust would required to develop a clear strategic vision and plan on the basis of which patients' care services will able to fit into the processes and priorities of the organisation on the operational basis (BMH, 2005). But one thing to keep in mind is that to design and implement vision which would enable the Patients' Trust to deliver and design care services for the long period of time.

5.2.3. Patients' Involvement

For the care services to be of high standards, it must includes the involvement of patients during the decision making process. The involvement of patients can provide crucial information and support throughput the care delivery process (Edgman-Levitan, Healing Partnerships: The Importance of Including Family and Friends, 1992). For this purpose the patients needed to be involved in the multiple levels. These levels are listed below:

i. Point of Care Delivery: The involvement of Patients at this level would assist the Trust management to analyse and assist the treatment strategies (Bohmer & Ferlins, 2006).
ii. Clinical Micro-system: The involvement of Patients at this level would be useful to plan, implement and evaluate changes (Coulte & Ellins, 2006).
iii. Organisational Leadership: The involvement of Patients at this level would be imperative to quality improvement and programmatic development.

5.2.4. Supportive Work Environment

This factor put emphasis on the creation and development of an environment where the organisation's human asset (work-force) is to be treated with dignity and respect by the Trust

Management and thus expecting their employees to provide same level of dignity and respect to their patients as well (Chapman, 2003). So in this manner the supportive work environment would be created and sustained over long-period of time (Rave, Geyer, Reeder, Ernst, Goldberg, & Barnard, 2003).

5.2.5. Systematic Measurement & Feedback

This aspect would contribute a lot to the existence of Robust Customer Licensing Capacity which would allow the Trust to measure and monitor its patients' care services systematically (Edgman-Levitan, et al., 2004). In this regard the Trust could use Balanced Scorecard which incorporates certain measure of Performance: Patients' experience surveys, Patients' Complaints and the Patients' Loyalty.

5.2.6. Quality of Physical Environment

This factor anticipated on various indicators: Enhancement in Clinical Outcomes, Patients' Satisfaction and Economic Performance (Pebble, 2006). One study has explained the characteristics of physical environment in an innovation way, which is quoted below:

> "It is considered as the therapeutics for the Patients, Supportive for Patients' Involvement, Restorative for staff member under stressful situation and efficient for the caretakers' performance."

> (Arneill & Frasca-Beaulieu, 2003)

5.2.7. Supportive Technology

This factor is linked up with the Health Information Technology (HIT) which could engage patients over the care process by having direct communication with the caregivers and also through the adequate access to the required information. The critical thing which is significant to this factor is to make simple adoption process for both patients and clinicians in order to offset the threats that the technology would weaken the quality of interaction between patients and caregivers.

5.3. Strategies for Leveraging Change

This section will highlight various strategies which would assist Trust in implementing Patient-Centered Healthcare System on authentic basis. These strategies are classified into two groups. The first one would strengthen the Trust capacity to accomplish Patient-Centered Care at the

Organisational level. And the second group would meant to alter external reward in the Healthcare system which then guided the Trust to achieve the delivery of high standards care services to their patients. These strategies are described in depth in the portion below:

5.3.1. Organisational Level Strategies

5.2.1.1. Leadership Development
This strategy is intended to focus on the substantial resources and capabilities of individuals to occupy this critical role (Simpson, 2000). In order to be successful it must include whole pipeline of healthcare leaders from all levels (Graduate to Senior). This strategy must be implemented on the cross discipline basis from administrative to nursing to clinicians and also span around the healthcare delivery sector (Firth–Cozens & Mowbray, 2001).

5.2.1.2. Internal Rewards & Incentives
This strategy must be pursued to assure that the care-workers are rewarded and retained on the basis of their performance of desirable level. In order to accomplish the successful implementation of Patient-Centered Healthcare System, the Trust must have to provide compensation and reward at all level of its operations (from the medical staff to the front-line worker).

5.2.1.3. Training to Improve Quality
In order put emphasis on all of their patients' needs the Trust required to train its staff member in term of quality enhancement concepts and methods which would make them to measure and manage change in care services in an effective manner.

5.2.1.4. Practical Tools
In order to begin the transformations towards the approach of Patient-Centered Healthcare, there is a desperate requirement for the Trust to keep track of that particular change in the form of documentation which then to be made accessible for the managers and change leaders. For this purpose, the Trust could use practical guidance which are to be based on the effectiveness resulted after the rigorous evaluations. In this manner, it would assist the efforts of its well-trained staff member under the supportive work environment.

5.2.2. System Level Strategies

5.2.2.1. Patients' Education and Engagement

This strategy determined towards educating and engaging patients to adopt the proactive approach over the care process and hence this strategy would be a decisive effort for the Trust to make itself more patient-centered (Hart, 2004). This strategy would also be useful in involving patients at the various level of decision making process which would then be resulted in mounting pressure on the Trust to be responsive to the need of all of its patients and thus intended them to adopt the patient-centered care approach on the continuous basis (O'Connor, et al., 2004).

5.2.2.2. Public Reporting on the Standardise Measures

This strategy would put more emphasis on the significance of systematic measurement & feedback to accomplish the objective of implementing Patient-Centered Healthcare System (Hibbard, Stockard, & Tusler, 2005). This strategy would not only be instrumental for monitoring and directing improvement in the area of care services but also making the Trust accountable about its performance through the public reporting (Shaller-Consulting, 2006).

5.2.2.3. Accreditation and Certification

The implementation of this strategic would put significance upon the external incentives for the Trust to improve its healthcare services on the continuous basis. These programs would build up the measures for the patient-centered care which would then permitted the Trust to prioritise and evaluate the delivery of services of high class standards which not only allow the organisation to deliver services of such standards but also stop them to deliver services which falls short of that particular standards (NCQA, 2006).

6. Conclusion

So it has been concluded the Trust must have to build consensus in implementing the Patient-Centered Healthcare System and also needed the special effort from its management and staff members in attaining the key factors of this approach at the organisational level. So with the successful implementation of this approach, there would be greater probability the system could do better as whole and also would able to improve the level of its care delivery services. The only challenge which would be faced by the Trust in the form of changing its current services' standards through the utilisation of strategies at both level (Organisational & System). But once these strategies would be executed in a timely manner then it would be resulted as the innovation which could be motivated the large scale implementation of this approach across the other institutions as well.

So in this way Patients' Trust would able to get rid of care service delivery problem and thus would intended them to improve their patients' satisfaction not only with their care but also with their clinical outcomes as well.

7. References

Arneill, B., & Frasca-Beaulieu, K. (2003). *Healing Environments: Architecture and Design Conducive to Health.* Francisco: Jossey-Bass.

BMH. (2005). *Bronson Methodist Hospital.* Retrieved March 13, 2013, from http://baldrige.nist.gov/PDF_files/Bronson_Profile.pdf

Bohmer, R., & Ferlins, E. (2006). *Virginia Mason Medical Center. 9-604-.* Boston: Harvard Business School Press.

Chapman, E. (2003). *Radical loving care: building the healing hospital in America .* Nashville: Baptist Healing Hospital Trust;.

Conway, J., Johnson, B., Edgman-Levitan, S., Schlucte, J., Ford, D., Sodomka, P., et al. (2006). Partnering with patients and families to design a patient- and family-centered health care system. *Background Paper for Invitational Meeting of Patient-Centered Care Leaders.*

Coulte, A., & Ellins, J. (2006). *Patient-focused interventions: A review of the evidence. .* London: Picker Institute Europe.

Edgman-Levitan, S. (1992). *Healing Partnerships: The Importance of Including Family and Friends.* San Francisco: Jossey-Bass.

Edgman-Levitan, S., Shaller, D., McInnes, K., Joyce, R., Coltin, K., Cleary, P., et al. (2004). *The CAHPS® Improvement Guide: Practical Strategies for Improving the Patient Care Experience.* Boston: Harvard Medical School.

Firth–Cozens, J., & Mowbray, D. (2001). Leadership and the Quality of Care. *Quality in Health Care* , 3-7.

Gerteis, M. (1993). *Through the patient's eyes.* San Francisco: Jossey-Bass.

Hart, P. D. (2004). *Americans and Their Health Care.* New York: Blue Cross and Blue Shield Association,.

Hibbard, J., Stockard, J., & Tusler, M. (2005). Hospital Performance Reports: Impact on Quality, Market Share, And Reputation. *Health Affairs* , 24 (4), 1150-1160.

Institute-of-Medicine. (2001). *Crossing the Quality Chasm: A New Health System for the 21st Century.* Washington, D.C: National Academies Press.

Institute-of-Medicine. (2001). *Envisioning the national health care quality report.* Washington, D.C: National Academy Press.

IPFCC. (2006). *Institute for Patient and Family Centered Care.* Retrieved March 15, 2013, from www.familycenteredcare.org

NCQA. (2006). *National Committee for Quality Assurance.* Retrieved March 15, 2013, from http://www.ncqa.org/HEDISQualityMeasurement/HEDISMeasures.aspx

O'Connor, A., Stacey, D., Entwistle, V., Llewellyn-Thomas, H., Rovner, D., Holmes-Rovner, M., et al. (2004). *Decision Aids for People Facing Health Treatment or Screening Decisions.* Chichester: John Wiley & Sons Ltd.

Pebble. (2006). *Pebble Project.* Retrieved March 12, 2013, from www.healthdesign.org/research/pebble/.

Rave, N., Geyer, M., Reeder, B., Ernst, J., Goldberg, L., & Barnard, J. (2003). Radical systems change. Innovative strategies to improve satisfaction. *Journal of Ambulatory Care Management* , *26* (2), 159-174.

Schein, E. (1992). *Organisational culture and leadership.* San Francisco: Jossey-Bass.

Shaller-Consulting. (2006). *Consumers in Health Care: Creating Decision Support Tools That Work.* California: California HealthCare Foundation.

Shortell, S. (2005). An empirical assessment of high-performing medical groups: results from a national study. *Medical Care Research and Review* , *62* (4), 407-434.

Simpson, J. (2000). Clinical Leadership in the UK'. .4(2). *Health Care and Informatics Review* , *4* (2).